MW01275498

Failing to Fall

James Griffin

ROADSIDE PRESS

Failing to Fall
Copyright ©James Griffin 2024
ISBN: 979-8-9905466-3-9

All rights reserved. Printed in the United States of America. No part of this text may be used or reproduced in any manner without written permission from the author or publisher except in the case of brief quotations embodied in critical articles and reviews.

Editor: Michele McDannold

Roadside Press
Colchester, IL

Table of Contents

To getting through it…
harder than you ever thought
but surprisingly achievable.

i will not fail to fall under the wheels of my life

tonight out in the
somewhere
the girls are playing again
the game we invented
for them
and if i feel better
later on i might toss
my ego onto the table
for luck
or maybe i'll just sit here
adorned with
my shorts and the
ease of apathy
but
i will not fail to fall
under the wheels
of
my life
i cannot wrestle
the angel to the mat
for a 3 count
or explain the permanence
of moments murdered
by a stranger
known as youth
only the photo
of myself and that girl
with a tiger stalking her hair
seems sensible
in the evening of continued
future uncertainty

two women on my bed
luck
tucked inside the waist band
this is the way it
will end and
i hope nobody minds

mahler please

she's mad
running into my room
i mean mad
just crazy
lost to the delusions
of our world
she could make
someone happy
wearing boxers
instead of panties
the quilt over my legs
was sewn by her
grandmother
and i look for
the madness
in the stitch
but
all i find
is the thread
so unlike life
straight and even

in the blue light

the seconds flash backward
on the vcr
and sometimes i don't
know
what to do with
all the moments
under blue lights
with breasts
and legs
all over me
wishing to hold
me
to cover
me
so much time
crushing backwards
instead of happening
forwards into the years

the hard luck will come for
me just before dawn
when i will be dreaming
of your pale puckered
flesh
so dirty milk truck white
hurling your thoughts
at the walls
and window screens
a post punk poet philosopher

the turn of a doorknob
or the stop light on 5th

which always takes too long
will bring it back to reality
the metal reaching forever around
us in an attempt to
become beautiful

like when i bled in your mouth
catching a glimpse
of the elusive melancholy
of your skin
once again
in the blue light
with pop songs
in my head
the cigarettes leaving
a trail

**logged in
(or streaming the conscious and failing
   the fast)**

put the thoughts to bed
6am i'll be on a tourist
modified and bleeding
wheeling toward the waiting
the jaguar stolen
on 18th st
by the laundromat
turning over
it all tumbles
by
while we wait

empty beds
in small rooms
a wooden suitcase
given by some
german girl
held everything i
owned
it wasn't so bad
cheap dinners
and cheaper
entertainment

now it takes me
the better part of
a week
to pack up my things
i wonder when i will next
maybe i'll see

brighton beach again
on a fall day
walk down coney island ave
and get a coffee
pretending that chicago
was a dream

hey nickey i remember you
on the boardwalk
in your vacay shirt
all red and pigtails
and a wedding
colored by your sunburn
me picking weeds
out of a walk
that's not mine

these and more
all drift past
images of what
has passed
little goldfish
in my smaller than
average sized bowl

2000 words

you are walking with boys
through streets i have known
in rain
in snow
and sun
covered fall mornings
sitting in a back garden
drinking coffee and feeling
the wind tug gently
as he is also tugging you
further along toward the night
across the street
waiting to tell you his heart
wanting to touch you
and tear you apart

the night feels itself september
and knows how to show us
glimpses of winter in its coolness

the cars are busy trying to get
where they have been pointed
music is in moments
like this
in you
a walk
with a boy
and in me
a man across town
giving up with little effect
small painted seconds slip
by without you

and resolve into
canvases of your absence

still
the morning will arrive again
the apartment empty
windows open to the breeze
and traffic
it feels good

flight & bliss

they take
pot shots at me
on the street
in the restaurants
as i drink
my coffee

but the spoons
seem to not be
as vicious
maybe they don't
really have the guts
to finish me
off

the waitresses glide on
and somewhere
toasters sigh
at generals
these weeks seem
to get better

the car is running
well into
the night
down the road
to st louis
into dreams
soft as books
smelling of
chocolate

i'm still
only a pawn
just away
from an english
opening
but perhaps
the blood in
the sink
will be
redeemed

perhaps i can
pull this one
out
and ride
past the whores
of history with
their bared breasts
ride into a
rifle tower afternoon
leaving the desperation
backed away from
my door
crouching in
the bushes

just waiting

gift-box phonecard

picture frames
and paper scraps
litter the
table the
way you
litter my thoughts

as tibet waits
in the corner
for
the sunset
for
the faltering
and for
the waiting
i'm halfway
on my
way
to you

the leftover
left to
endure
like miles
to lassa
the roof of
the world
it lies
pink between
your robes
i'm yet to
tire
of the
climbing

east coast rising

floating on asphalt
under endless skies
through
stretched out parcels
of golden topped
green
each
separated by
small twisted hurts
music
turning on a
tape deck
the wind carries
it up, out, and away

i stopped to pick
wildflowers
for a celestial
beauty
held hostage
by central state
institutions
unaware
in a few months
she'd never come
home again
lost to
the east coast rising

until then
it was late nights
spent laughing

in diners
clubs
hot wax in bedrooms
drives into st. louis
the deserted
streets steadied
by her trusty
gas station gulp
filled with a potion
for bravery

madness

i don't understand
don't think i will
ever
understand
all this madness

women sitting
writing, studying
flying to new york
and not coming back

phone calls
unmade
hanging between
states

the driftwood thoughts
gathering in
my shallow memory

i was 2 when
my sister led
me onto the roof

later she
pushed me
into steps
blood covering
my eyes
in a church

looking up at
stars

through a cracked
windshield
on my way
to the hospital

when i was 5
i learned to tie
my shoes
taught by
my father
drunk on cheap
schnapps

he beat me
until i could
tie them
like a man
later that week
my mother started
up the car
and killed our kittens
who had crawled up
near the fan blade

we hid on the bluff
away from the coyotes
watermelon seeds
growing in our
bellies alongside
the fear

fear of blood
flowing from burst
ear drums

fear of the small
bus and smelly
driver
fear of this
madness

but there were also
afternoons
laying in bed
listening to jazz
coleman hawkins
or lester young

tracing my finger on the
headboard
watching my father
absently twirl
his hair
as he read a novel
and waited for me
to drift

there was no anger
there
or in the light
playing through
the sheets on
the clothesline
as we ran through
the wind
gently wrapping
the corners
around our laughter

watching the crawdads
in the stream
ready to scream
and run
the cold water
and warm air
a glorious mixture

the hot asphalt
on cold feet and the
warm air turned
cool as we
got on
and pushed
our bikes through
the world

in the end
i guess
i know
it takes these
things
moments and sweetness
to keep the madness
at bay

i want to be the pencil in her hair

the other night i heard a man page
my name in the peanut butter aisle
under dull mass manufactured
increased pocket emptying
economy boosting senseless
pop tart, dannon yogurt
(what no banana man?)
buying inducing fluorescent lights
so i floored the boot drolics
of my turbo trixie amped
shiny disease ridden
shopping cart
and made like maddened
pigeons to a baptism
for check out lane #7
and
there he stood bearing
a pistol grin
with all the avid apathy
of a generation without a cause
or emotion
plastered inside out
on his name-tag heroism
winning anonymity

well now i'm as groovy
as the next cat
who has enough self respect
to still play colecovision
shunning this new
lipstick slick prepacked
slacker technology

80s buck rogers (don't forget twiggy)
and friends but this guy
made me think of
gummy bears getting tattoos
what?
i'm in trouble now
in the dying evanescently
evanescence of his personality's
mid-wife crisis
hope the lucky strike holds
while someone hands me
a twisty tie elvis
complete with super 70s
rhinestone napkin cape
the muzak whines kentucky rain
through smoke swirls of
jerry mourning hippies
bruised battered & abused
but no worse for the wear
go ahead
try one on
inside a denny's all american
i think this guy's gonna be my friend

sweet bird of youth

the first flush
has passed
and
now past
i have retained
myself
to small rooms
w/butterflies
where baseboards
and doorframes
weep white
waiting for
a tinny electric
voice
over a battered
bronze box
death is a mortgage
like a grey cat
striding
patient
toward your lap
turning black
shapes
a distraction
and a comfort
open mouths
and heavy breaths
piles of white
and ink
on the table
questions and answers

do the streets
remember me?
as they lie
across
the belly
of a belted
and bibled town

unbalanced load

who will
tell the tulips
they are alone
who has the
courage
to tell
this person
they are
unheard
in
mid sentence

once
it would
have been you
once

when you were
still hurling
your bike and body
off of mounds
of packed dirt
when you were
bored bothered
and quoting
action movies
or
just after driving
down the
hill in your
first car
or maybe

even after
the first
embrace
her smell
still damp
upon your
unbelieving
lips

you could do
anything
then
but not
after that
because
then
roses became
supermarkets
roses became
an afterthought
like a
candy bar
courage
became obedience
to the dollar
to the schools
to the professor
standing in front
of your resignation
standing like a
monotone madman
secure
in his clothes
comfortable

standing in
his shoes with
no support insoles
dry smile
after dry smile
a slow turn
of days
turning
late nights
to early mornings
on time
clocked in
present
but maybe
even then
you had not
given up
perhaps you saw
the professor
and he
stood with
a different madness
behind his
eyes
like a beast
screaming
for your
soul
perhaps
you saw
the urgency
of knowledge
come upon
you

and maybe
you took it
to your pocket
and secreted
it there
nourishing
it
with small
apples
of art
and literature
yet
as the
years passed
that small
thing weakened
in your pocket
next to your
manhood
and became
just as
unimportant
until one
night outside
a laundromat
as the lights
played about
the clouds
you saw
everyone
else like
cardboard
glued to sticks
and pushed

around
your reflection
caught in
the floor to
ceiling glass
another piece
of stiffened paper
and you
almost
did it
you almost
walked
out of it
away into
the streets
with everything
behind you
the gnashing
teeth
of lighted
signs
loosened
and let free
your flesh

instead
you bowed
down to
the guns
leveled
at your
heart
and
put another

quarter
in the machine
and
come friday
someone will
have put
another quarter
into you

332 canal

sparrows weep
but seldom
under mosquito
netting
we lay on
bamboo
italy four blocks
away
china
even closer
the air an
animal
stalks us
there
till slipping
to slight
slumber
we enter that
listless purple
sleep

among the jellyfish

what is
it
beyond windows
and
rice paper
brooklyn
a white washed wall
4 miles to the
ocean
left on the
beach
among the jellyfish

2 hours past
a russian dinner
with an italian
a chinese
and me
left on the
beach
among the jellyfish

i have waited
on the breakthrough
of the d train
over the east river
some post icarus
flight
putting the light
into morning
eyes
i have waited

wanting
stripping down
the doorway
for phone calls
from chicago
there above
remembered fence posts
across
fields and furrows
and
mulberry lanes

left on the
beach
among the jellyfish
i think of scotland
and of the french
meat
pictured in books
on her floor
she left me like a
motorcycle falling
to yellow

left on the
beach
among the jellyfish
thinking on korea
as she wakes
with a daughter
here
sleeping
and caught
in the opposing

magnetic fields
of our hearts
i am afraid

beautiful 8

maybe her name
was latin
for temptress
and maybe
i should have
noticed
the dogs
turning away
as she passed

so dogs
at least this
once
were wiser
than me
it's true

i should have
realized
the seashell
smile
she gave
when we embraced
was like a
leopard
over its kill

instead
i saw
february afternoons
blowjobs on the freeway
and a

body walking across
my room
in the half light
of hope

dogs:8
me:0

one bullet

there is death
in the kitchen
and
there is sorrow
in my belly
for the mother
next door
who lives a life
like
dripping faucets
running toilets
monotonous
mad
she confesses
with the fury
of ants
cold beetle stories
of youth
run from her tongue
into my ear
she shakes and cries
for lunch line ladies
missed sunday sermons
and the man
who stopped
one afternoon while
the children were
at a school
as my arm finds hers
i commit with knowing tone
another friendly fatality
"it'll be alright"
the stains are brighter than blood

it's really something

the way the rain
hits the glass
at 11am
to watch the people
run
a butter blond with a
volvo man
watching the rain
chase them like fear
like judgment
mindless with society
and the voice
of the man on the radio
"punishment" for our sins
weather weapon of
god

well
i don't know
i think that
he's far from
here
and "mother" earth
is a bit much for me

it's really something
the things we believe
because we're told
to
the words we utter
in hope of control
control of

our cars
our mates
our jobs
our friends

it drives us to murder
to petty moral victory
to government
and yes
it's really something

as this mutha
gets out of his truck
shoving the rain aside
with slow sure steps
of disdain
he strides in control
of what he can control
him
his grizzled face
and dirty clothes
shove society
down the throats of
the dogs
where it
belongs
and i'm
better off
because of him
and the rain
and the impossibility

fix a flat

the run of
cold luck
like flat tires
near beauty shops
gnaws at my mouth
turning the corners down
still
i salute
all the pain in
the world
for its ability
to carry out its
duty
day in
day out
day in
theirs is a job
i have neither
meat nor meter
to master

10 steps

that's all
i could manage
12 just
seemed like
nonsense
i think i
would rather watch
tv
or listen
to a record
there are enough steps there to
keep me occupied

first i had
to plug in
the motorola
a big
70s console
version
i bought it
at a
salvation army
for $15
it came with
a captain and tenile
album
and
a sister sledge
lp

if i wanted to
listen to a

old 45
perhaps
clarence carter's
"devil woman"
or
maybe a
hasil adkins 7"
i would
spend a good
5 minutes
deciding and
then
looking for the
little spinneret
thingy
to enable my veneered
beauty to even play it
turning on the motorola
was always a
happy moment
hearing the
tubes
warm up
watching
the turntable
grudgingly begin
to spin
then
after a short
skirmish with
my clumsiness
i would
get the record
on

i've always
loved watching the labels
turn
little pieces
of art
and lovely

of course
there is that
moment
of anticipation
as you
lift the arm
and place
it
as delicately
as possible
on the vinyl
i don't care
what you are
into
be it pills
drink
or whores

there is
always
that sad
quiet
moment
before it
begins
that moment
when all

your fears
and hopes
for the feeling
to follow
are distilled
into some
immeasurably infinite
space

savings time

cambodia
is nestled
with my
friends
on our couch
3 hours ago
we lost time
to a war
over 50 years old
i think
we used to kiss a lot
now we make sure
to brush our teeth
and lie with smiles
even still
i try to catch the truth
of you
with words written
in slanting lines

nafisah

have i ever
sung you a
love song?
because you
are beautiful
like the aegean
(that's a sea)
because i balance
on concrete
walls
to see you
smile
and to feel
the fall
the falling that
never fails
despite
me failing
to miss a step
and even
though
it will be
almost 3
years in october
i have yet
to teach you
chess and
i have never
sung you a
love song

still
we make

love to
and
uphold
great standards
on rainy
afternoons
that smell
sweeter than
flowers
still we untwist
words and
laugh while
i kiss your back
we have greeted
each other on
misty mountain
mornings
in pennsylvania and california
we have held
each other
on coney island
i have watched
you sleep
through big
texas nights
as the
diamonds sparkled
on the windshield
we have eaten
ice cream in st louis
forever caught
in a
photograph
you simply smiling
making it all

worth the while
the whiling of days
away
in the streets
of chinatown
the late nights
waiting
in front of
apartment buildings
in grocery store
parking lots
in chicago streets
all is left
waiting next
to your eyes
and your cheeks
even wet with tears
in moments of
small hurts
i can't help
but admire them
i can't help but
sing
even though
i have never
sung you
a love song
you are music and magic
walking through
twilight
richer with symbols
and meaning
than any
celluloid dream

she writes

everybody writes
poetry
i
write poetry
badly of course
the grape jelly
is gone the way
of bullfighters
and hemmingway
because
books burn easier
than gold

guns lay
hot and naked
next to hands
on carpeted floors
and
roses fool the sun
while i wait
against the window
and the telephone

solitude
comes only in crowds
and small birds
reaching for the roof

we had a deal
or so she
thought
yes

we did
locked in water pistols
set to
shoot out the
horsemen
only getting as
close as the
bush

so i'll sleep
in my car
again tonight
hoping the police
won't catch me
and
the dandelions
won't blush
as the oceans
sit on the world
so very far
away

midwest untitled #00026

sick with 7
nights
on the couch
empty photographs
of you
destruction
huddled under my
left arm
voices rarely
make people
sound closer
to lucid

your silence
was the loudest
thought
ever uttered into
the soft
crackle of
15 states
between us

a week later i
wake with
fear
in my right
hand
like a gun
like an alarm clock
like the absence of
you

midwest untitled #00013

11:36pm
on route 36
just past mile
marker 78
the dragon eye moon
lazy and orange
looks down on me again
for my tomorrow
another start
of another beginning
to occupy my
hands and mind
so recently
fallow of feel
i will hold a pitchfork
on the roof
of a church
fighting for balance
i will break
its skin
revealing the reasons
until
your foot follows
water on a bathroom rug
until
we both cover smiles
dancing our eyes
about the room
and into each other

12:27am
the turn onto route 67

is accompanied
by the dragon
slanting to angry
as the night begins its
fall to day
the moments
pound my body
melted by months
of missed mornings
next to your
stomach
scarred
and your shoulder
rounded into mine

12:38am
the headlights
and the rear view
make my eyes
a bandit
as the stars
open up to
reveal themselves
a tiger
in their
distance

from the king of nowhere

8:57am
snooze button stuck on
serendipity
the quick leaning on the razor
burns my throat
leaving the blood
in the sink
i am out on the sidewalk
past the bent and broken
bench
before
i remember my daughter
in bed
turning on the light
she greets me with round eyes
full of sailor moon dreams
i dress her
over protests to blue
her morning goes south of my
mood in minutes
then car is filled
with her stare and hair
and lip
that sit behind me
and to the right
all she wanted
was the white vinyl shoes
so seemingly sensible
to a 9:15am 4 year old
heart

9:30am
my rear view filled with her fickled
face
i'm ready to concede
9:45am only an
hour late
losing more respect
than money
the day files past
pleasing until lunch
trying to dissuade
my memory of a morning
misplaced
and white vinyl shoes
left by the bed

1:15pm
cover the phones
deal with the dealers
lie to the unknowing
kiss a bit of yourself
full on the lips
and lay a five
on the nightstand
as you walk away
working so hard
to become consumed with
consumption

5:15pm
traffic is not a fight
you don't fight it
you lay back
prone eyes

glazed as glorious
jesus golly
glassware
and you let it assault you
like this i have
become
numb
in no way comfortable
lessened by the closeness
of society
standing still around me

6:30pm
checking the pot pie
i burn my finger
the 4th one
right before the pinky
it brings to blister
my skin
stretched by the faintness
of feeling
the evening sits on
my shoulders
for the next several hours

9:20pm
television is fastly
fading from my
feigned interest
the radio plays
the love songs
of the lost and lonely
in vain
turning me

to pictures of you
on a pier
all teeth and eyes
and cheeks
full as autumn apples
but your laughter
has been lost
for months
lasting longing
to limpness
with thoughts like these
minutes run marathons
in their passing
and coffee's black bitterness
becomes sweetness
to my tongue

11:05pm
i lay on the couch
waiting for the rest
of the wicked
and as the ceiling
dances to the bass
of the people above
my fists clench the sheets
showing someone
somewhere

12:05am
the phone rings
"what?"
a woman on the other end
says
"do you believe in beauty?"

the subtle shudder of the sparrow?
the green valley viewed from above?
the whore in that yellow dress
on south 14th street?
or maybe the invention
behind your smile
the roundness of your
body brought full with our
daughter

the 4:00am fury
of a woman standing over me
shouting to be heard
above my indifference
and yes
perhaps the leaving that
left me clutching the phone
like a lover
turning words to weapons
to win a battle i thought
i had already won
only to realize
in the absence
of your brush
and your silence
i had ransomed
the queen of my heart
to become
the king of nowhere

brit pop

i saw a sunset
red clouds
laying across
the trees
my hands
dirty from
two hours in
that apartment
on 11th street
and i was
resting with
the sunflowers
against the wall
in the shade
lorries and planes
underneath my hair
tea rolling
to and from
a little room
somewhere
southwest
of usher hall
where behind a
door and a wardrobe
there hides a
brit pop queen

nyc untitled #0005

on carmine
past the noodle shop
walking west of here
brooklyn receding
i can't get you
out of my morning
because two nights
ago
on the floor
westminster road
just north of coretelyou
i found your breath
with mine

alley

her bad episode
re-run laugh
hits me under
the eyes
before i can duck
into my smile
headlight moment
between us here
too many stories
winding up the key
to my life
she looks under the lid
and pulls the cord
laughs and lies
lies for laughs

midwest untitled #00037

the paperback
is there on the
edge of the bed
disturbed by my
interest

we leave passing
a octogenarian
wearing his
broken
colored dream coat
staring under the
street light
at a puddle full of stars

of all the gifts he wore
around his neck
under a smile
and above his
heart
understanding
like a chair back
angel dance
is not easily
received

so in passing
we passed
all the years
he had bled
oblivious to the
dreams he had dreamt

and made our
way into the
false prophecy
of another afternoon

3:12

if all the wars
were fought
so i could lay in bed
at 3:12 this afternoon
then they were
worth all the death
because i've written
3 poems so far
and i think
for days
like this
even god must
get jealous

black beans and corncakes

the old men
have gathered
at my tables tonight
alone and assured
it has made the
last two hours bearable
those hours
have passed
like glass barbwire
smooth and clean
instead of being ripped
from my back by
hateful fists
there is only one
hour left
and the special is sold out
i don't think dante
could have imagined
an inferno as towering
but
if i can make it through
then maybe
i can stave off god
and religion for another
week or two

between france, ireland, and
   afghanistan in chinatown

i was staying with an ex girlfriend w-
in chinatown nyc
the evening was dead
hot and silent
sitting at the small kitchen table
we ate noodles
not talking
looking at our coffee
currently i was infatuated with a girl
in scotland
she was finishing her mfa
we sent each other postcards
i had one she sent of ferdinand celine
a mugshot inset with a picture of some
building
he had lived in
i really liked that one
she was to come to new york
in only a few weeks and stay with me
once i got my own place
i was very excited by this
people knocked on the door
and we opened up
it was an irishman and a french girl
the irishman was a friend of w-'s
the french girl was his ex
in town to visit from paris
this was an inconvenience
he was living with his current girl
in brooklyn and she
was very cross

so in the interest of young love
i was to stay at the place in brooklyn
whilst
the french girl was to stay with w- in
chinatown
i forget his name and hers for
that matter
although i do remember her face
and how her name moved around in
my mouth
almost like it was alive
it made my tongue work
and my lips stumble
it's better forgotten
we went out to some bar
in some part of that city
all of us talking and drinking
me on the soda
around 1am we were in hells kitchen
and some girl gets up and walks over
to me
she knows someone in the group of
people
around me
bad music was playing
perhaps a cuban jazz influenced hip
hop
the lights were candles
the drinks very expensive
this girl wearing a tank top with no
bra
as her nipples eyed me she smiled and
pointing
at my t-shirt said

...i'm from chicago too....
the fluttering of her lashes
snapped something inside
...that's nice for you...
i turned on my heel and walked out
into the night
i thought of the little round girl in
scotland
i wrote poems in the air
and in the gutters
i sat on a curb and thought about
motorcycles
falling under cabs on church street
about the girl reading my poems
at some dank pub in scotland
i thought about the distance of an
ocean
and of all the voyages that had been
undertaken to overcome it
just as i was being overcome
by people and that city
w- walked out and trying to reach me
she stumbled down and to the left
hitting pretty hard
she is bruised and limping
and so incredibly red
she always turned red
about her face when drunk
angry and ugly like some great fever
out of a russian novel
we half walked
half limped to some all night
jamaican eatery in the west village
we ate and i began talking

very stupidly
about love and humanity and
dreams and hopes and fears
these moods come over me
especially late at night when out with
strangers
who are drinking as i am not
somehow w- made it off
and i was left with the french girl
and some other irishman
a friend i take it of the first
irishman
he had been chatting up the french
girl
all night with marginal success
i had seen some kisses and awkward
gropes
exchanged under muddled lights
now in a cab we were trying to get
back to chinatown
the cabby was an afghani nationalist
in the states to raise money for
friends back home
he became involved in some debate with
the irishman
and as they argued the french girl got
closer
and closer to me
and somehow her hands were on my legs
and her mouth found my neck
the evening opened up into a new place
my poems to the little scots girl
came back now to my mind
only they were read by a girl in a

paris cafe
on a fall afternoon
she found my mouth and worked into it
i tried to say her name
and it made my tongue work all around
hers
she was now straddling me
her hands underneath my shirt
lights were exploding somewhere and a
young girl
was getting up to go to her morning
classes
on a cool scottish day
i pushed her away
the irishman and afghani had become
very quiet
the cab had stopped
we were in front of w-'s apt
the french girl asked if she could
come up
of course i told her it was not
possible
this made the irishman happy
she would be at his place tonight
his rebound odds had just skyrocketed
i went up 3 flights tasting french
lipstick
and expensive vodka on my tongue
i fell to sleep thinking again of the
girl in scotland
and dreamt the dreams of the righteous
and the fidelis
a week later the girl from scotland
wrote me a note

describing her involvement with a
young curator
and how she would not be coming to new
york
i had spent several more nights by
then
with the french girl...talking and
having coffee
she had left the day before i received
the note
she had tried several times to kiss me
and i had refused
citing my young scottish lass
i guess the only lesson to be learned
is
that like the germans in the forties
we must all
take paris while we can

chinese charm

tonight am i in
your palm
circled round
precious
perhaps
like a charm
or
does the night
tend toward
industry
with bird like
persistence
its distant and
easy flow
belying the burden
of your cheek
in hand
neither lithe nor slender
yet more graceful
than a willow
weeping upon my window
as the chestnut
warmth of your skin
lingers more
than memory
with the missed moments
moving through
your eyes
somehow almond
and listing into
the emptiness
of a second floor apartment

with an uncovered
couch
and water falling
on the bathroom floor

wrong time fever blister

the impossibility
of a cat asleep on
your lap
has driven me
into the madness
of cars and people
and lights
and lines
and waiting
next to polished new
fresh white smiles
like great jagged
rocks
at cliff bottom
miraculously fitted
into mouths by the
millions
now i'm just waiting for
the shove
in my back
but it won't come
not sudden and true
and honest
no
instead
there are nudges
from family
and friends
and everyone
like taking out
the trash
it's steady

...unrelenting
death has patience
equal to salt
and snails
she
will sit in languor
as i slip
against
the wrong corrected address
once again
and somewhere
god still hasn't stopped
fondling the angels

**taken to the church of i do not want
   what i have not got**

a skinny kid
driving a broken car
parking next to a pizza place
up a dead end street
the buildings a mix of
prefab and 1800s brick
skies open
and reaching
a tableau terrible

yet
with her voice above
somehow it
all seemed
less mean
and small
touched by the gods
she touched my dreams
as they unfolded
across little towns
amidst
dirty little apartments
made light and large
with her melody

yellow dress

the tongue
in the mouth of
the cobra
has been tricked
into venom
just as the
angel inside
my head
has been lured
into iniquity
laid out
back bleeding
onto unchanged
sheets
the stink of
17 women
riding tricycles
around my belly
above the
bounced check of
manhood
true yellow dress
days
were lost
long long ago
under a tree
safety pins caught
under the skin
sticking our moment
to just a moment
we left it there
as we drove

to work
and easter sunday fellatio
but this angel
he still glistens
with fear
of yellow dresses
and what they held
for junkyard twighlights
never quite
forgotten
armies march into
the womb of history
bred into words and books
and legend
and culture
and pride...and shame
but mostly pride
while only you and
i will clutch at
that afternoon as
our souls
slither up from
our toes
over our hips
through chest and neck
to hang feverishly
onto our eyes
and lips
but in the end
we will fall into
the air
and the sink
will glow with
unfinished dishes and broken promises

halstead northbound

my life
is a slow burn
cautiously catching
the city
it sits
behind me now
a shadow
its breath
reluctantly rising
wandering to become
lost
in this winter white
the ear of van gogh
has made its
way to me
via trails
and rails
and bicycles
on freezing dark
mornings
the blue has turned
to red
on the side
of my head
throbbing
swollen and ugly

flight 39 SEA --> LAX

do i look defeated
do i have the taste
of defeat to your eye
if so can i take
that defeat
and make it an
air to fly in
crowded full
of others
as they
fall through
i'm angry
and scared
looking for
a place to
land

left

left right
left of right
left of the
right of
way
near here
left there
listening to the
absence with
a pop song
the bowery
is a street
and a city
with coffee,
convicts,
parks,
and waiting at 1:00 am
chinatown sleeps
with whiskey on
her breath
where it's 20 mins
to brooklyn
and believe me
leaving me
is all the rage
along bridge and tunnels
still with this
pop song

15 and life to go

i am left in a city
that is not my own
clarity will not come
but waits
it is said
behind locked doors
for years
and regret to fade
with blood in the sink
your voice has
taken me from myself
books on the mantle
a girl's silence hung
beneath
innocence is a slender
thing
slipping too quickly
away
as i drive
my car
in a perfect
movie montage
moment

deeper shade of soul

fucking in sheds
hungry hands
hunting and hurting

rings thrown off that bridge
junkyards filled with
steam
and our bodies

a fine brown frame
on a blanket
watching christmas
movies

we were crazy out
of our heads
with
lust and laughter
loud sex
your family in the
next room

sweet dates with dinner
and movies trying
to understand ourselves
having sex in the gym
skipping typing class

getting caught
in a car in a field
windows wet
and clouded

by the
cop who had just lectured
your class the day before
oh and that bridge
i was jumped by that
bridge
while your little
brother looked on

so many stitches and
broken teeth
laying in the ditch
the snow so warm
and comforting
as the boots kicked me
in the head

they were pretty surprised when
up i jumped
hitting a few
pushing another
i was off up the hill

some miracle of
something...

first love
turned to longing
lost nights
shouting
and that poor
kid
who took you to prom
rolled up in

a rug
found by the lake

you raising a child
off to california
then more children
and too many years

i went a little bit
more crazy

rolling
around in a 5.0
listening
to the ghetto boys

i took a soldering iron
to my arm to wave
off this girl
named debbie

shortly i ended
up in another
mustang
kidnapped and hostaged
to my heart once again

memories of the mound

slipping through the illinois morning
flying like an eagle in the back seat
of my parents' car

on my way to an ancient burial mound
rising up out of the river bottoms
the missisippi mud holding lives in
reserve

i'll eat cold meat
out of a tin
covered in syrup

these things sickly sweet
memories
pain and pleasure
in equal counts

playing with broken toys
in dirty goodwill aisles
2,000 miles and 40 years
later i'll watch my boys
do the same

it's all luck
and
i've had a bit of it

burgoo beats

pleather fingerless driving gloves
closed at the back
with velcro
young men strapping
fresh and fecund
full of
mirth, anger,
cruelty and
sometimes on
a sunday
a bit of kindness and
contrition

tiny ferris wheels
creaking and groaning
in spite of all the grease
and oil
whose smell hung in the air
every revolution
a hour of terror
wondering if this
tired warhorse could carry
you through

skinbird rising

punching meters
was easier than punching
nazis
giant posters
misfits & dead kennedy's
music played on a little
fisher price record player
electric frankenstein
seen with a lesbian
in some nyc basement club
the sweat and the movement
i lived there
beneath the public
swirling a small
pool amongst small
pools
a lonely current
running through
catching coffee
bitter and sweet
on corners and sour smelling delis
the clock always
counting down
stickers of small children working
in mills
"it's coming"
the message was mine
and i still don't know what
it means

10 mins to freedom

i sit in a car
listening to dead singers
singing dead songs
sung by my grandmother
everything is a poster
an ad generated
glistening garish in its gleam
but
bad art is better than
no art
let your
existence be
art
live into the day
through the night
letting it all
in and putting it
all out
nothing lasts
like a memory
and even
those are
fleeting

champaign

into the night
slight with flowers
chrome gleaming
up and down
market aisles
me dreaming of z-
and the time
we battled with
toy swords
through the sleep
and pain of youth
spent
only small change
left over
for 2am forays
into all night toy stores
you bought your
gifts
and i smiled at the teller
skinny and awkward
i followed your cracked
lips
smoothed over by
petroleum
into a chain cafe
to drink not
spain from my cup
but rather some poor
third world country
down in two gulps
as smoke crept
from your mouth

and crawled up your nose
a snake after prey
and you said
hello to a friend
half a world away
because the full moon
reminds you of
an old chinese story
about a boy far from home
i listened as you
described it as a
snow star kind of thing

it had been such a long time
so i cheered the waitress
so i looked at you
so i derided the boys 3 booths down
so i opened a book
so i read to you from fante
looking for the understanding
in your expression
four years from now
will i be a half a world away
saying hello to you
through the moon
turning to the one
i am with saying
have you ever read fante?

for jen

i lost 3
bets to get
to you
stranded on an
island
of well wishes
onlookers
confused and
a tiger stalking your hair
punk rock prom
was chesterfield kings
in some house
somewhere
i remember
a basement show
galen screaming
you showed
me propaghandi
and left me
wondering
last time i saw you
in that upstairs
shop
skank skates
second floor
did you
make that m.d.c.
show?

midwest untitled #00256

looking back to kisses kindled
on summer evenings
in lonely cornfields
i touched a russian princess
then got out of the car
and screamed at the moon
i must have seemed ridiculous
or terrifying...
pretty sure i jumped off a bridge
next to a rumbling train
a few weeks later
trying to drown out
the sounds behind my eyes
my body and limbs
notes of a life floating there
each liquid vivid and clear
reclining into a simple phrase
i still have not made matter

mbamba bay

we walked down the red clay road
the children swirling around you
the smiles and laughter lifted
the warm air holding it closer somehow
not letting it go

the joy was pure and infectious
you raised your camera
and they posed again and again

a game that didn't seem to end
the steady click of the shutter
click
click
click

as it went on the air became hot
the laughter and smiles glared
hands began grasping

perhaps we were play things
being derided
and perhaps we would
soon be broken and discarded

before that could happen you slipped
away
you have a knack for slipping away

down the dry mud hills over roads and
tracks
to lake nyassa's edge

a town of concrete slabs and
corrugated tin roofs
behind us

the sun glinted off the water
and the lake sounded a murmur
constant and soothing

your hair streamed golden and brown
the wind flowing around your
skirt cooling the air
we talked of something
i wish i could remember

the boats were black shadows
on the twilight shore
you focused your camera on the
wooden dugout canoes

i think it was to do with school
yeah, we talked about schools

i think

the smell of the fish didn't register
but the hundreds of eyes on silver
slashes
pinned through on drying racks made of
sticks
brought me silent

they were an excuse
i think we argued

we probably argued
we usually argue

the sun had left and our steps grew
slower
the air chilled and made me shiver
we walked the beach until
the great grey elephant rocks heaved
themselves
up at the end
blocking our path

place your bets on the sunset

death is a stop light
red blinking busted
confused and asking
what is the point
or the reason
or the foolhardy
plan of it all

to be born into
streets and slums
or fields and flowers
to be born into
beasts and blood
or computers and cars

picking up a paycheck
for picking up the trash
hard nights in cafes
waiting on the lost
and listening to their
pain
place your bets on the sunset
for it always wins
no mean mug
can outlast the
blast of death's final blow

let the flowers die
and let the season end
place your bets on the sunset
for it will all begin again

slipping through the
air flying on two wheels
past lights and moments
missed and missing

stopping on a gravel road
to pick wildflowers

riding the a train from
harlem
as a wisconsin family
gets a taste of
the masturbating
madman in the next car

driving 16 hours hard
through the night
the mountains breaking
into morning as you
push over the top

the smell of coney island
late at night
the city a backdrop
and the coldness of the water
turning the air

countless cafes
cars and coffee
memories made
and marveled

kicking out hard
in a st louis club

free in the room
with music and mayhem

kissing a girl in
the junkyard
kissing a girl under the
el in chicago
kissing a girl in chinatown
in new york
kissing a girl in the middle
of a midwest field
kissing a girl in a motel
under a sisters of mercy poster
kissing a girl on the roof
of an art gallery
kissing a girl on the beach
by the sea
kissing a girl as prince
plays the last notes of
a song left over
kissing a girl before
leaving and never coming back

place your bets on the sunset
it's coming and will not
turn aside
for you or for me

place your bets on the sunset
but
take all the moments until it happens

midwest untitled #00079

today
i thought of you
of your cheeks
of your worried
smile
i thought
of your lips
and eyes
quirked in
childlike mirth
raised in the
soft comfort
of the country
i now find myself
surrounded by
the hard city
and a cool wind
the lack of wanting
is only replaced
by jealous needing

trakking the horizon

riding by rail
past industry
and its
sun dappled
and dilapidated iron
resting amid the flowers

the capitalists sing
"look at our progress
look at our production
we make it
we buy it
together we can
run to the future
kissing cares
goodbye
with lipsticked
dollar signs
we can make
the lovers laugh
with bubble gum smiles"

and all the while
i sigh and sigh
looking for the exit
getting down
over the barbed wire
and freeway miles
closer to the slumbering city
second only to
the beast in the east
and the cotton mouthed
king in my chest

poem never written

the coldness
of you
the anger
of you
is cheap gutter boy
emotion
that leaves me
tired and more overworked
than all the
jobs i have ever had
with the darkness
of night sitting
on my ability to sleep
go away
go
away
leave me in
control
of the light switch
in control
of my doorway
your hand forever
absent
from my skin
this is not
happy
nor encouraging
in the silence
between the sound
of your feet
moving outside my door
lessen my worries

by thousands
and
don't speak
or cry
or smile
or laugh
or explain
again
please

spaces

i am best in spaces
small and barely
containing my shape
but my
headphones still fit
loneliness still fits

here in these spaces
my children walking away
disappointed
knowing that has to be ok
to retain this feeling
on top of my fears

failing to fall
under the wheels
of my life
is a continuous
and tenuous effort

all the bills and the
opportunities are piling up
stacked in neat rows
"i'm really impressed"

i am best in spaces
internal and large
where the landscape of my
life is infinite

i fought dragons
on a paper route

through midwest winters
leaving the blood
on a garage door handle

they were easier to
slay than my responsibility
so many mouths and others' dreams
small stones in my pockets

here in these spaces
i rebuilt the shelves in the
garage
the driveway needs a dry well
it's slowly sinking
under the weight of doing
the work

the rv across the street
has some young kid
ready to cross the country
only he has lost his cat

he has been there three days
he needs to leave it
and move his space

i want to grab him and tell him
to move his space

i am best in spaces
to the side of yours
just out of reach
looking into this store windowed world
i can live this life

the revolution is internal
the flag is still waving
on my arm through the nights

i am best in spaces
barren and cold
the window open
the breeze the breath
of life
falling in

the dogs are running again

the dogs are
running again
tonight
near a corn field
across a gravel road
sun dappled trees
lens flares
and echoing voices
just like the movies
boys in blue jeans and
white t-shirts
girls in little dresses
all of us laughing and hiding
in the corn
the soft silk and the
sharp blades

there was a barn
full with hay
or straw
a vast cavern
gaping cool
black and calm
sun pouring in
through the cracks
teleporting the dust
there was a small blue cat
a pin
whose face opened up
to reveal
a mirror and some balm

the dogs are running again
tonight
towards a funeral home
next to a roller rink
it had the biggest puddles
when it rained
i would jump across them
i would jump in them
brown and murky
they were lagoons
and lakes
and oceans
i sent fleets
to their doom
upstairs there was
an attic
i read comics
above where bodies were embalmed
i couldn't read
but i looked
a box of them there
i never knew where they came
from
or where they went to
my father gave me my first
taste of beer in the
viewing room turned
living room
i didn't like it
that has stuck
i haven't drank one
since

the dogs are running again
tonight

towards a small ramshackle grey house
set on a hill in the country
we would walk down the gravel
to the crick
go wading for crawdads
i would follow
my brother on his bike
he would tell me
nervously
breathlessly
"there are wolves across that field"
he would dare me to go
i would go
my heart in my ears
and my little fists clenched up
he would tear away then
laughing
leaving me in a field
surrounded by grass taller than me

i played with my sister
among sheets and clothes
hanging on a line
we would try to climb
the septic tank
we would eat mud
on graham crackers
we would hide next to the furnace
when pop got a mean drunk on
we would cry and listen
my brother just sat in his room
thin and taut

i would lay in bed
with my father

as he read a book
listening to jazz
he would curl his hair
around one finger absently
over and over
i would trace the intricacies of the
headboard and fall asleep
twisting my hair too

we had to get water
from town
on the back of a truck
to put in a tank
for drinking
for bathing
mom would pile
us into the cab
and turn it over
once it made a loud thumping
noise
mom and my brother got out
to look under the hood
finding my brother's cat
in the fan cowling
a small puddle spreading the dirt
mom tried to be strong
reached out a hand
laid it on his shoulder
he just hid his face in
his hands

the dogs are running again
tonight
they are tearing around

slavering for a piece
of the sweet meat
i'm laying here
remembering all these things
offering them up

kissing cousins

1964
the streets straighter
than a jacket
korea was a dream
vietnam a
growing nightmare
he could tell a story
and i could hear them
he could laugh
he was cooler than
jazz
cutting up
the court
at the back of the
bar

she's got a razor
and he's got a piece
facing 10 in the
pen
he found a preacher's daughter
to ensure parole
and she became
a canary
blood from her
ear
but she got him
back
50 years later
he woke to
find his feet
had taken a walk
don't underestimate
the power of doing naught

square life

orange and warm
the soft yellow
glow of the radio
i'll hit 60 eventually with finn in the
back, the road
guides me through
pines, cedars, and firs
a quilt with varying shades of green
dead singers are
singing dead songs
bits of chrome
reflect the land
making us a mirror
as we roll
next to lakes
and streams
the burble of the
flat four
blending the rumble
of the asphalt
and the wind

framing a moment

soft light
falling over
faded red
cloth
above it your
apple red
and rounded
cheeks
smiling

giving love to
the best boy
his body
all movement
and joy
that cannot
be contained

i'm content
to watch
from the next
room
at a remove
reminded

reminded
of the fall
of the love
and of the joy
all my own
contained

olympian banshee

that bike is
at it again
loud obnoxious
tense and terse
a wrung out
engine
screaming through the
punishment
as it wails down
the road

like some mythic
banshee
heralding darker
times
it flies past
the house
disappearing into
the night

my nerves settle
creeping back
from the edge
into their bedclothes
turning to thoughts
of otzi the iceman
frozen in the
schnalstal val senales valley glacier
how did he die?
what pollen gives us
the dates for his life?
tiny instances
of time preserved in...

screaming back again
comes the torturous
whine
flying through the air
ripping the night
shredding my nerves
and leaping through
my brain
as it feverishly
strains to not
overheat in rage

no small part of me
keeps hoping
for the inevitable
crash and smash
the symphony
of metal and glass
spewn over asphalt
soaked in oil
and blood

lest ye be eager

i fell and broke
my wrist today
pulled down a hill
by a dog
too eager for the
trail

it sits here
in throb and
groan

tomorrow i'll probably
see the doc
after i wind
out the morning
in the woods

letting the dog
pull me along again
the air will do
us both some good

by train when available

broken battered and blue
those fingers holding
the page like a
cigarette
tender cool
caring calm
and callous
all at once
the words smoking
and drifting
out of your memory
here in our separate
present
i'm reading about
our separate past
wondering
simply
what's going on

i'm not telling you a secret

everyone knows how bad it is
the broke down mornings
the almost wrecks
the 8 lbs up on a random machine
i hide in the closet
lest i let it tell me
more often

west coast untitled #00082

the house is quiet
the kids out to a movie
i'm drinking coffee and
listening to jazz
missing my mistakes if
i can
as the day is
tripping to tasks
left undone

honda ct90

we bought two ct 90s
off a hippie named max
his girlfriend was set free
in the 70s
we drove a van past
military surplus
you tell me
there is an artist
in la
who takes pictures
of stop signs
and painted crosswalks
just so
his clothes always covered
in paint and his words
covering poor passers by
his house in brazil
bought by his parents money
the rain patters
painting the screen
we missed the turn
and he missed the point
of the revolution
which probably won't come
or probably will
i mean it's a numbers game
and i feel the odds are getting
short
it's a 20 min drive
home and chet will
play the way
scoring your

chatter which i used
to stand and now
i savor every word
maybe you'll see it
the revolution
coasting into
our world
wide and wanton
before anyone notices
maybe mike will be
on one of the ct 90s
outrunning the gunning
or maybe it'll still be cold
and broken in the garage

how many moments

from your sad eyes
how many words
until i am removed
from the kitchen
overflowing with dishes
the dust piling on the books
how many reasons
before your shining black hair
is lost to the dark shadows
of trees and fences
i ask not to know
but to ask
the light dims
the air is cool

the old gym

smokey wood
shining and surrounded
by rough cinder blocks
pickle ball courts
dividing the space
a hand lost to a
combine doesn't
seem missed as he's
sending missiles past
my head
the tinny
sound of bad 80s
metal is ringing
out from the
stage
played on a tiny
walkman by
a rage filled
walking acne
commercial
in a room filled
with people
sweat, fear, and
polyester
my only companions

heavy lift

the geography
of the moments
we have traveled
falls across
america

we should post it
on the bedroom wall
driving pins
into the points of
interest

the north side of chicago
where
we met
the jesus short
order cook
telling truths into
the morning

that cold basement
where
recovering from
a crash and custody
i cut together
the moments
of african immigrants
while you held a microphone

the dark studio
where
we made out to

the sound of a gay lover's
story
set to rain
under the elevated trains
where
running lines across
the city
you wore some frilly
skirt an attempt
at pretty
and i drove you more than a
little mad

the south side
where
you drank through
one christmas
12 inches between us
each inch a mile

in some park
where
frozen by a photo
you are pregnant and smiling
on a playground
toy
purple pushing across
your belly

the great plains
where
rolling endlessly
by the window
we watched them

pass
as the babies cried
and only luna
soothed bewitchingly

the mountains
where
wet and frozen
all at once
in 3am
darkness
dashing up and down
knuckles clenched
i dove us into
tomorrow

i90 west bound
where
breaking into
morning
the green was
everywhere
and life
lifted us

14 years later
we drove to lunch
on my 50th birthday
in a 72 vw
playing music from
the 30s on the am
radio

time has cracked open
and spilled
across our life
disjointed
moments mending
moments

left locked
alone in a green impala
with a white hot wheel
waiting for her to come back

replaced by legs and arms
intermingled
whispered words
jousting
with loud laughs
and a dog melted
into my butt

the long arc
hopes toward happiness
but if i'm honest
your smile
has done the
heavy lifting

slicing the vertical

i take care to
pay attention
to the in between
to the dull rhythm
of the rain on the gutter
a flat hollow beat
atop the uneven
staccato
to those faces
unsure
uneasy
and waiting for me
to stop talking
the tense and
heavy moment
before walking
away
the swaying trees
in the distance
and storybook
skies
just behind
the stop light
the laughter
of everyone gathered
in the next room
as i'm staring
at
the peeling paint
here above the
door i need to fix
our son asleep

on the couch as i
slip into the kitchen
to sneak a bowl of cereal
at 1am
i pay attention
trying so damn hard
to not be relegated to
just the
in between

art for david

i see them
the artists
in the galleries
in the paper
on the television
saying this is
ART
and the girl
the boy
on the street
walking by
believing
it

getting
hooked in
falling for
it
like religion
like body blows
buying it all

when
the real art
is the
auto mechanic
the real art
is the subtleness
the knife
in the waitresses
smile

unwanted alliteration #00076

turning tickled
tortured tendons
toward tomorrow
i can do it again
i'm sure i can
i can make it to morning
mended and marveled
gazing once more into
the maze
my feet feeling
fleetingly for yours
luck might
lob us some love
leftover from
late nights
lost in loose sheets
laughing
it will be enough
to push and provide
pink prose
as it grows
meaningful with
our mockery of the marketing
as we meander
making moments
in the market

colons copy

the waiting
eyeing the seam
in the wallpaper
the repeated
conversation
the same interaction
transferred to
different people
behind green
curtains

the waiting
looking at beige
instruments
and purple tubes
alone
why are there
so many lost moments
waiting
alone

i am past prime
and still anxious
i want you
here
to talk about
the bent metal
holding the
stained ceiling tile
in place

the yellow room

textured walls
floating under
a white swirling
patterned ceiling
so much movement
and light
making me sick
with a desperation
to see the valley's
end
to watch the clouds
contort and build
to follow a road into
the distance
leaving behind
the quiet tension
razor wire
waiting
to be tripped
the screaming and gagging
the boy pistol
whipped at the table
"steal another penny from
me and i'll put a bullet in your
head like you're a fucking puppy"
the praise jesus sundays
followed by
praise jesus wednesdays
interspersed with
self righteous sinning
with hapless
clasping at

ideals in need of a laundry
walking
biking
driving
training
flying
all means of egress
have been attempted
and achieved
even boats
but those left
me wallowing
stuck mid stream
on a sand bank
littered with
debris
years later
striding
mountain passes
poised so close
to their imagined
heaven
i almost felt far
enough
safe enough
to release these
memories

for buk

it's wednesday
and i'm feeling surly
driving is a mental
gauntlet
behind the old man
in his powerful and polished
new machine
he's too scared to drive it
inching along like
maggots on bones
too afraid
of his insurance
his health
or the ticket
waiting around the corner
like death
and i'm as bitter
as the child with a
cone
ice cream melted and gone
no understanding
nor caring for
why these things are
just content with my
anger
sitting close as an angel
and if this is poetry
then i'm finally saved
and bukowski
i hope god doesn't have
your soul tonight

i get nostalgic at night

i send you poems
written about safety pins
in white crumbling
farm houses

king of new york
playing via an ancient
vcr in the front room
on repeat

the furniture made from
beer boxes
someone was always
drinking mickies

we were just
on the right side
of the tracks

but the cops still showed
up and
the walls still
got caved in

i think i stayed with
you in a weird loft
style apt

i remember butthole
surfers being popular

i had a job cleaning up

a restaurant kitchen one night
i didn't even understand
how i got there

literally i don't know
how i arrived at the location
or why i was there
or if i ever got paid

i stole this girl from
a guy named drac
made a joke and a move
and that was it

found out she was
15 several weeks later
when she asked me to take
her to school one
morning after sleeping over

tonight i'm with myself
listening to music
and memories

the girls are distant
the woman i married
is comfortingly close
in another room

it's a far better thing
than i could have hoped for
and most would say than
i deserve
perhaps even you

easily bruised

you have a red vacay shirt
or you did
in that picture on
coney island
pigtails and wind
beach and boardwalk
ocean and smiles

you drove way too fast
on back roads in
central illinois
sometimes with me
gripping anything
i thought might save me

we went to an underage
club in some town
and they played
sonic youth
the only song
i could dance to

there has been
a conga line
of men
snaking in and around
your life
i was in there
somewhere
pretty bad with the mariachis

you rocked a lot
and thought about life

maybe we argued hegel
or maybe we
talked kant

we definitely sent
missives like missiles
lobbed cross continent
an explosion of joy on
each receipt
our life made
better by the blast radius
of our friendship

6:12 am

the light sits
golden on
the green
edges
of the trees
pasted onto
a pale
blue sky
laying quiet
next to you
i hear
the blackbirds
roaming as
they
call and cry

the town is
rousing to
the morning
evidenced by
the sounds
listening like
a lawyer
i count
the number
rising
of cars
going by

your soft snore
a distraction
countered by

the contoured comfort
of your warm skin
where my fingers
trace patterns
following your form
living lifetimes
in these moments
before the day
begins

1958 schwinn corvette

cruising to blue
flying through
the night
a streak down damen
following the moon
and crossing the el
at lake

the air is only
cool if you're moving
don't wait for the lights
the holes in your hands
are because you tried to
think

forget about the man against
the fence
frog marched through
the snow
to a waiting escalade
on christmas eve

wipe the blood
away like sweat
grit and push
this is summer
and
the city
is an open
opportunity

a third floor
walk up with

semis floating through
the living room
windows

a small park
pressed onto
chinatown
a view of
railways
reaching into the sky

18th street
a hustle
holding us all
with its warmth

pastor at coyote
laughter coming easy
banda on the jukebox

tall bikes and cans
on display
as the punks joust
for fun

pop pop pop
"fuck, he shot me, he shot me!"

i should get out on
the freeway
and point it south
back it down
to the deserted polish
towns

boys running through the gangway
caught across
the street
and beat

latino groceries
saved parking
spaces
more aunties than
i can count
making menudo
and lighting
candles for all the
bad decisions
forced upon them

we started a family
there
among
a few small houses
one rented to us
by the cabbage

treedrive

left solitary
in an empty space
the pounding of the neighbor
dictates my sleep
you are northbound and angry
little reminders
of our love
a constant thorn
in a place you cannot
reach or remove

it's christmas with two trees
a hedonistic whirlwind
gluttony and love
all flowing
one into the other
and back again

is there a ship to point?
have i foundered on the shores
of happiness and content?

i'll walk the dog in a bit
his black bumbling bulges
running and falling
bounding and crashing
into everything

on a sunday

she stirs in my lap
chirping and purring
a great white cat bird
of legend
masked in black
so many claws and teeth
scratches and kneeding
laps and turns
nuzzles and bites

her so busy in her wanting
i so perplexed
in my clumsy
attempts to fulfill

finally she settles with a
long stroke from
ass to shoulders
repeated and repeated
her paw reaching out
and clawing my forearm
her tongue making
appearances as well

finn looks on from
the floor
great sad eyes
accusing
he turns with a huff
and lays his bulk down
staring into another room

west coast untitled #00306

left with you
left in the kitchen
i have found
the right place

cats run crazy
small hissing
streaks

dogs hurling
themselves
after everything
large black shapes
of
muscle and joy

ticking of boxes
and writing it down
the feeling is still
there to
write it
down

it's not for you
or for anyone
just for the
writing it down

east bound flight

3 hours in the air
over america
it's maybe halfway
turn the tale
to tragic
as small bits
of atmosphere
drift below
woolen white wisps
weighted down with
worry
kong fights a giant tiger
in white cotton tableau

straight flat fields
turn to gentle curves
as the river rides
into the valley
the trees follow
gentle swells and
the undulating earth's
irregular character
making the story
told over millennia
plain and easy to read

the clouds are
hung like paintings
above the gravel pits
the houses and
lives so ordered and small
this height cannot contain

the enormity of the
next door neighbor's brother in law
layin hands on her
nor can
this remove
reconcile
the heap of blood and bones
of my son
thrashing out against this world
his mind
a bouncy house
in a warehouse parking lot

out of the past

i turned left at chicago
and kept going until
i arrived in the place
you were born
i have never felt as comfortable
as in these
verdant valleys
and
calm shores

one day your name arrived
out of the past
like some noir
mitchum moment
filled with fear and excitement
it had been lurking in
memories
and boxes
dusted over and put
away

i am feeling through
photos
your body and your smile
the freedom of youth
reaching out into the
future
blowing the dust
off these fine forgotten frames
showing that age has only
burnished them
brighter

time has dulled the hurt
and the blame
leaving the small
perfect hope
of our bodies
coated in sweat
and intertwined
on
yellow dress afternoons

found objects in manila and plastic

today
i found poems
in a folder
full of photographs
scribbled scratches
slanting down
and away

trying to recall
when and where
i wrote these
thoughts
and then
put them
there to stay

but there
were so many
days, nights,
and afternoons
full of fear
and feeling like prey

they run together
in a pack
of memories
the only thing
falling behind
stumbling free
is how hard it
used to be
to see tomorrow
from today

the boats

i flew across
the east river
in a tube of steel
breaking brooklyn
mornings
and iron moorings
still in a submission
hold from a childhood
1,025 miles away
fleetingly feeling
freedom amongst
space
sky and sun
arcing out bright
shining above
the water
an arrow
silver and true
all too soon
returned to quiver
pulled back down
to the waiting maw
toward tunnels
burrowed beneath
a city never asleep
up again
into bustling streets
past doorways
with belts for sale
bodies pressed
close close
and closer

creating steam
forming afternoon
dreams
of
escaping
out through
twisted tiny
alleys
arcades and shops
restaurants that
don't accept cards
across
brick paved parks
full of motion
and thrill
only making it as
far as the
grimy theater seats
4 blocks away
where
the god of gamblers
laughingly
held sway
liberty is glanced
and stolen
in fevered gasps
a midnight kiss
from paris
or
slipping free on
the ocean's edge
with the jellyfish
perhaps
still

we're all enclosed
and slowly
eaten by
our
fearfully near
and oh so distant
past

ten floors down

silence follows
toward tomorrow
as the sky's fall on the
horizon
with the red apple
color of autumn
and this
bed left empty
gazing at windows
facing windows

silence follows
russian revolutionaries
fading after
long distance
calls finish falling
on ears
and
silence follows
little laughter
from jokes
sitting on the couch

waiting...

clean up on aisle 12

there is so much love
spilling out of her
it falls on the cats
turning them
sideways elongated
stretching
to receive it
i trip over it when trying to
get some coffee
falling face first
into it
surprised and a little better
for it

there is so much love
spilling out of her
it surrounds our
sons
buoyed and bobbing
warm and comforted
they float through
a world that is
filled with it
never to
not
know it

there is so much love
spilling out of her
the dogs cannot
drink enough
she is a wet willy

water bug spraying
all over their lives
belly rubs
rolled eyes
and afternoon naps
they dance and tumble
drenched in her love

there has to be some
trick
to all this love
i keep watching for it
trying to catch her
out
filling up
restocking the stores
instead
she's doing laundry
or
nuzzling a good boy
or
laughing at a 6th grade joke
or
looking through lego
for hours
or
calling the insurance company
or
gently humming a
song as she sits next to
me

there is so much love
spilling out of her

i am awed by its
volume and form
i have been so
covered by her love
it has filled me up
to bursting
and by some
strange turn
love is now
leaking out
of me in small
drips
forming puddles
that might catch
you too
if you're not careful

romantic proclamations of affirmation

these are things
i say to you
or try to
on a regular basis
i hear they are important
and i was raised to
pay attention
to everything as if
it were important
lest i get a smack
about the head

frustration
is easy to
come by
like pennies on
a dresser
ever present and
unsurprising

less common

is cool air coming
in the windows
as we glide along
the small town road
listening to chet
or coleman
or duke
or ella
the point is
the radio sings

the evening is before us
and my heart is full
and my head is working

working out all the wonderful
things you are and ways
you affect me
i consider myself a dab hand
at turning a phrase
but
the volkswagen keeps
us close and
the closeness is driving
me crazy
i cannot think in a line
down the straight street
i am jumping and
swerving to the music
of the radio and our
love

i want to pour it
out of me
cover you in my
happiness
with clever phrases
playfully joined
hinting at things
hidden to most

all i manage to say
is
"romantic proclamations of
affirmation!"

in a voice wholly too loud
and oddly enthusiastic
you respond by saying
"don't yell at me"
but
you don't smack me
about the head

almost blue

always looking
for my life
i found it
but it's not mine
tone on tone
the notes
fall
in strange phrases
coming up
major
where I expected
minor

years spent
in rooms
windows opening
on walls
in cities
hot with summer

motels next to
cornfields
kissing christian death
until I was blue

south side
night rides
losing to
the tracks
bloodied bitten
bruised

no heat novembers
cold showers
a can of soup
per day

have resolved
into a comfortable
home
2 dogs
2 cats
2 children
and a wife
in a town
nestled tween
mountains and lakes
lush and green

chet plays
his mournful
melancholy
melodies
that don't fit
the scene

part of me
is still expecting
it
but seems
I may have finally
learned to
fail to fall

Publication Notes

Special thanks to the editors of the
publications in which these poems first
appeared.

Poem Alone: "clean up on aisle 12"
Red Fez: "2000 words"
The Beatnik Cowboy: "one bullet"

Raised in the river valleys and
open fields of central Illinois,
James Griffin has roamed and rambled
from coast to coast and beyond.
A punk rock poseur, and armchair
anarchist, reaching for the roof
he has landed here.

MORE ROADSIDE PRESS TITLES:

By Plane, Train or Coincidence
Michele McDannold

Prying
Jack Micheline, Charles Bukowski and Catfish McDaris

Wolf Whistles Behind the Dumpster
Dan Provost

Busking Blues: Recollections of a Chicago Street Musician and Squatter
Westley Heine

Unknowable Things
Kerry Trautman

How to Play House
Heather Dorn

Kiss the Heathens
Ryan Quinn Flanagan

St. James Infirmary
Steven Meloan

Street Corner Spirits
Westley Heine

A Room Above a Convenience Store
William Taylor Jr.

Resurrection Song
George Wallace

Nothing and Too Much to Talk About
Nancy Patrice Davenport

MORE ROADSIDE PRESS TITLES:

Bar Guide for the Seriously Deranged
Alan Catlin

Born on Good Friday
Nathan Graziano

Under Normal Conditions
Karl Koweski

The Dead and the Desperate
Dan Denton

Clown Gravy
Misti Rainwater-Lites

Walking Away
Michael D. Grover

All in a Pretty Little Row
Dan Provost

These Are the People in Your Neighbourhood
Jordan Trethewey

They Said I Wasn't College Material
Scot Young

Radio Water
Francine Witte

And Blackberries Grew Wild
Susan Mickelberry

Licorice Heart
Miles Budimir

Disposable Darlings
Todd Cirillo

MORE ROADSIDE PRESS TITLES:

Full Moon Midnight
Belinda Subraman

Innocent Postcards
John Pietaro

Cistern Latitudes
James Duncan

Another Saturday Night in Jukebox Hell
Alan Catlin

Abandoned By All Things
Karl Koweski

Ain't These Sorrows Sweet?
Lauren Scharhag

Gregory Corso: Ten Times a Poet
Edited by Leon Horton

She Throws Herself Forward to Stop the Fall
Dave Newman

We Don't Get to Write the Ending
Aleathia Drehmer

These Many Cold Winters of the Heart
Ryan Quinn Flanagan

Things You Never Knew Existed
Josh Olsen

Maze
Jennifer Juneau

Green Roses Bloom for Icarus
Hiromi Yoshida

MORE ROADSIDE PRESS TITLES:

Let the Scaffolds Fall
Shaun Rouser

Apocalypsing
Jason Anderson

The Things We Tell
Sara Glasser

Made in United States
Troutdale, OR
11/08/2024

24329937R10108